Dedicated to all the souls who unchained themselves, because they dared to give credit to their dreams and findings...despite of being called crazy innumerous times

# STARSEED RECALL ON BEING HUMAN

## Rants of an alien waking up

**LAURA PIQUERO**

# TABLE OF CONTENTS

## Introduction

*Hi. My name is Laura, I was named that by my Earth mother during this lifetime, but she said she was dwelling between that and Alejandro if I would have been born a boy. Laura represents "Victory". Since my life on Earth has been a constant battle against the current until I woke up, I am glad her genes aligned to birth me a girl.*

*I was born in 1986, part of a template called the Indigos or according to XXI Century humans: The Millennials. For what it's worth, we came here to break all the rules, coming in waves ranging from the linear time of 1950s until late 1980s to restore the sovereignty of the people. We hold a signature in common: the codes of not conforming, holding rebellion in our veins which is gracefully balanced out by die-hard empathy (which makes us extremely vulnerable to human suffering and other people's pain). It's what they would call down here our GPS, that marks the north when it comes to staying*

1

focused on the bigger picture, despite the immediate circumstances. However, having this gift can be very confusing, we are not exempt to drowning in pain whether it is foreign or not, and that lingering over-absorption feeling, often times leads to a prevalent yearning to check-out and abort mission altogether (if you know what I mean).

My first remembrance of something higher than being human, was marked by a letter I wrote to my earth mother around 7 or 8 yrs. old where I said: "Thank you for letting me know I was adopted". We had argued over something and that had triggered a response along the lines: I know this shit is not real haha let's take the mask off! I am not adopted, our resemblance is pretty self-evident, as well as the one I share with my almost inexistent father in every picture, but I just knew...I knew they weren't my "real parents". Shortly after, they divorced and I took comfort in the terrestrial pleasures that lead to pain and back to pleasure again:

philosophy, alcohol, astrology, sushi, making out, boy bands, neo-punk, dancing, yoga, writing, painting, and so forth· Unfortunately, trauma is one of our first codes to awaken· From then on, I alternated between the destructive human behaviors of the lower self, and the pursuits of the higher self: where metaphysics was so delicately intertwined among the fabric of it all·

I held great reverence for polarity at a young age, although I never actually committed murder or anything like that, I was simply fascinated by the idea of destruction, transformation and rebirth· I strongly resonated with the Indian Goddess Kali and with Lilith (the primordial woman)· Upon taking up the archetype my higher self-crafted (The Queen of Duality) in order to fulfill my mission of walking others through their personal underworlds too, I realized nothing had been random in my life: not the grief, not the pain, not the empath trait, not the deep-thinking quality, not the consistent abandonment· It was all there to help me hit the pit first and later assist others on their personal battles as they too faced change, transition and fear, in order to experience emancipation and retrieve their ability for wholeness. This I knew, was a huge part of ascending as a collective, purging all that crap with not "mindfulness" but rather with reactive Inner Child Therapy and Primal Scream Venting with undying support by your side, a healing companion if you must (that was me).

So it is! I have reached the Earth age of 32 and heading towards the completion of something grand in a year, when I will reach my life path number 33, the path of the Ascended Master. It is now the year 2018 and I have been waking up for a while now, to this knowing that life as we know it down here in these bodies is about to radically change. You see, I like many of you, came back on mission to help catapult the last days of a dualistic Earth and assist with the transition of a $3^{rd}$ dimensional planet into a $5^{th}$ dimensional one. That is why I felt drawn to

4

*leave these last 3D memoirs, because I just have this feeling, this knowing...that very soon, we will have forgotten completely what being human was like· Don't worry, we'll get to keep the glories of pecan pie and spring flowers, but the outrageous feeling of enslavement down here from money to common rights, let's call it a day with that, shall we?*

## The Tower Crumbles

*Humans breathe their way into complete physical birth, they experience cold, hunger and heat· Nurture and neglect play a part in their development, and the rites of passage from childhood to adulthood bring with them all forms of burdens ranging from hormonal dysfunctions, to growing pains, leading to burnout adults with too many responsibilities and very little room to be and enjoy the wonders of all that useless "hard work"· Forced to live in all forms of unnatural ways, confusing honorability with subservience, and at the center of it all: trauma, catalyzes the grand awakening·*

*Waking up was traumatic and it came in bouts that lasted over 10 years...*

*I tried for a few years during my early deep questioning process to verbalize the internal destruction, but words could not suffice· I was just on one of those roller coaster rides mentally, jumping from one page to another of* documentation, hidden meaning, synchronicities: anything I could visually grasp and analyze from alien races to vegetarianism and everything in between·

I had the same coping mechanisms other humans did: music, alcohol, busying myself and social interaction, but mostly felt withdrawn from the world around me, too immersed in my world to cohesively participate in the one that was presented to me· Likewise, I stared dropping the structures that didn't represent what I felt to be true on the heart level but couldn't argument why: the first institution being religion, which was challenged by the fact that I was raised under a Catholic faith and decided not to confirm my vows at the age of 18· What followed was dropping out of college, both formal (journalism) and artistic (performing arts)· Motherhood and marriage led to important questionings about myself as a woman, independently of the roles they wanted us to play and a few freelancing years later I was craving self-employment like the only sustenance towards real freedom and joy.

Jumping in the see-saw of disintegration and reprogramming that came after periods of clarity and vibrations of oneness, my older acquaintances started being replaced by true tribe members who were waking up to the fact that life was not what was being told collectively, but something more that could only be measured one experience at a time (bringing with it millenary wisdom), something magical and woven that had always existed and was just waiting to be tapped on. At some point I realized that although we could not yet talk to everyone about these remembrances, it was important that we found ways to tell our stories, in whichever way we were being guided to do so at the time, because these stories had codes of awakening and the truth indeed, had many forms (depending on the level of consciousness).

Past life confirmations and karmic catalysts later, I was sitting on the verge, hanging onto

8

the mental games of a malignant narcissist who aspired to torch my life to ashes· It was a battle for life itself, once I encountered a master of the dark arts which presumed victimhood at his earlier stages of grooming· It was truly the removal of the veil (this initiation) and the beginning of true immunity against all forms of manipulation· I had such clarity about who I really was, I was ready to take down the government from within, why? Because the power lies in dismantling the lie, the abuse and the corruption in whichever form it comes about· Unfortunately, it is not until we have witnessed the great evil down here in the form of someone who appeared normal, who we trusted, and who used all of our conversations to gather ammo for a later attack, that we are able to stop fearing the dark forces that govern this planet·

The void was imminent at that stage, my intuition was activated only to find that there were very little people I could trust from then on· The more light that was bombarded into the planet, the greater the outbursts of empty vessels that were wearing masks their entire lives· The minions of PTSD left me crippled for a while in the form of artificial walls: I craved connection, but interaction terrified me, solitude gave me panic attacks and too much stimulation left me drained· I would sit outside and wonder, how did it all end? I knew the end was really going to be the beginning for lightworkers and the only chance for peace, so I pondered many days and many nights...about what I wished our world would look like· What if we could? Build our personal utopia, and what if it all began at the mind, fueled by the heart until it erupted in the physical?

I jumped back and forth between the 3D (3$^{rd}$ dimension of physical matter) and 5D (5$^{th}$ dimension of unlimited possibility and co-creation), in the form of taking temporary forms of underpaid employment and participating in social gatherings of intoxication, as well as full withdrawal from them and into creative pursuits *like writing and painting which reminded me about the power of a pen, or a brush for that matter· I felt it as a form of grounding, but less and less was I able to stay in that state of survival for a prolonged time· I wanted to wake up every day and feel safe in the world, that no corner was restricted, that no neighborhood was dangerous, that no food was negatively charged, that no house was owed and that learning was just a way of life, while we collectively kept harnessing our specific roles in our communities and being of service with our gifts (without having our own needs depleted by subjects like taxes and rents); just free and loving exchange·*

*Less and less I was able to tolerate discussions about 3D matters like politics, religion, feminism, disease, education, and Christmas leftovers· They all seemed absolutely irrelevant to the yearnings I was having about New Earth and the unfoldment of a prosperous time: where self-governance was the main structure along with collaboration with others· One thing about awakening is, the earlier stages are all about attempting to prove to others that your information is real, but at the latter ones you will not cast pearls before swine because you learn that you have nothing else to prove to anyone· Call it the earlier stages a form of strong attachment which helps to cope with letting go of the obsolete reality, while the rest is more about: detaching from what isn't and allowing only for what feels right· You are now ruled by an internal knowing, not by the inner-child wounding seeking acceptance from others·*

*And there I was, detached from what had been, undergoing full rebirth myself and waiting for the great big change...human body or not, but nonetheless: ready for change· Make me come back as a free bird if you must, but free at last·*

Invasive Medical Procedures

*One of the greatest traps to keep humans enslaved was to use the tools of advertisement to sell them the primordial concept of: health· This was noticeable by the growth of "healthcare systems" where people were encouraged to pay a fee for "future protection from illness or speedy service during disease"· For the areas of the planet where this "service" was provided for free, people were encouraged to enlist for all kinds of benefits like "free vaccinations" and "free medication", which mutated the universal template of health the soul carried, leaving after effects of losing kidneys over migraines as well as destroying the immune system with heavy metals like mercury fillings·*

*The health campaign was also backed up by the top universities who sold the "medical profession" as a lucrative career· Via loans that would take a lifetime to repay or incentives like scholarships and grants· More and more people dreamt of wearing a white robe as means to* have a formidable future and a prosperous one (under the pretense of wanting to save other people's lives)· Insurance companies also played their role along with pharmaceutical companies, who sent out their young reps to form bonds with future doctors that would receive a commission: when the doctor prescribed their patients some of their "test" medication·

Plastic surgery was an undeniable way to rid oneself of "imperfections", although in some instances it did facilitate the lives of heavily injured patients like burn victims· And soon enough, it also became a way to alter the body altogether in the form of conversion surgery, jumping from one gender to the other one· From not so innocent needles infused with synthetics, to actual coma induced thorough operations, the Operation Room became the ultimate meat-chopping-fluid-sucking establishment, whereas the Emergency Room, became a place where people were asked to fill hours of paperwork in order to be followed by innumerous testing, *while undergoing a medical or health emergency.*

*There was an alarming increase in people not being happy with who they were, what they looked like and growing ever more powerless about taking care of themselves, starting with basic things like their nutrition, mental health and emotional well-being. Not only was this race for the perfect race encouraged by retouched/airbrushed magazine covers, but by social media filters and celebrity fandom. There were even reality shows that encouraged people to have surgery upon wining a competition or to look like their favorite TV star, like the stellar MTV show called: Made. With that of course, came side effects and lawsuits of people that had placed themselves under the operation table only to find that the facilitator of the procedure was committing medical fraud, using non-sterile products or trading breasts for limbs if it were the case.*

*When the medical system couldn't profit out of people's insecurities due to the increase of* lawsuits and expensive health insurance, the rise of entities like Herbalife paved the "more natural way", which consisted of signing people for a lifelong codependency on "natural" product. This new niche of "wellness" came accompanied by other minions like personal fitness trainers who would ruthlessly charge their struggling clients big sums for helping them "achieve their optimal body weight", turning human bodies into genetically modified organisms. With "wellness" becoming the new-word-on-the-web, people became more concerned with starving themselves through thin-hood and pill-popping themselves out of body weight, which in earlier times enabled Vikings to survive heavy winters. Empowerment coaches spoke about the next big secret to be "Happy", and older modalities of healing that were used by early ancestry were revisited and even re-sold at fashion stores as part of a new hip thing to own: like a bar of organic cocoa butter with sage and stickers.

And when it came to being healthy, food became

*a discussion topic too. Fast food was scrutinized, although almost all the human food supply had been contaminated by then by the Master Geneticist Monsanto: a privately-owned corporation who had all the rights over the basic seed of all nutrition, which via treaties of presumably free commerce trading managed to colonize almost all the countries in the world. There was a battle for the private rights of the entire water supply of humanity, which was for the most part already filled with toxic chemicals with the objective to rid the world of their people, leaving the 1% to enjoy the remaining beaches, waterfalls and the exclusive high-rise condos that no one working under the minimum wage could ever afford.*

*The medical entity was the beginning of our battle for survival, where individual awakening into the codes of self-healing was the only way to become healthy, happy and sovereign once again.*

## Humans Find Relationships Via Apps

*Courtship has greatly shifted from the times of sending written communications to lifelong lovers, separated by war...*

*With the worldwide spread of the internet (artificial intelligence that connects people via videos, texts, songs, emails, chats, forums, etc·), online "dating" has been popularized as an efficient way of accessing other strangers that are equally rushing to find someone to mate with· At first it was a convenient way for people with "busy lives" to rebound out of their lonely periods, failed marriages and even test the waters because it guaranteed there were: plenty of fish in the web· Entire businesses were built to meet this primordial need by providing interactive dating services, some at the cost of a small fee and others at a higher one that came with more personalized offers based on thorough psychological examination, which ensured higher compatibility options·*

*The sites also honored individual preferences ranging from religious beliefs (Christianity) to food preferences (veganism) and some were even up to the task to arrange entire marriages for complete strangers· That's right! You want to see what your destiny holds? Just give your credit card to an arranged marriage platform and you are sure to find "the one" on the hands of an expert, upon exchanging chat messages or clandestine encounters with strangers you are matched up with called "blind dates"· What was interesting about it was how the sites started breeding all of these hybrids· People wanted more and they had less time, so it ended in "simpler" ways of mating like: "giving a like to someone you found attractive based on their picture and ten-character bio"· And Tinder was born: an application that could be downloaded via an online store for free, which provided access to people in surrounding areas via their pictures, your task? To swipe over as many profiles liking pictures or passing by them with no reaction, until someone liked your picture back and Tinder* celebrates it by saying "match"· Then it is up to you to go out with the person and actually weigh if you can "make it or break it" or just stay swimming in the sea of online flirting, getting nowhere concrete but gaining a lot of fans who don't even know if that's your real picture·

What followed or perhaps what was hidden until Tinder, was Grinder: an application where no fucks are needed to express "you simply want to fuck", as equally emotionally disconnected as the MOB (Male Ordered Brides) structure in which humans are able to purchase a wife from another country through a website, and have it delivered to them via mail (plane, train or shipping container)· It is merely a form of Black Auctioning out in the open and without protection from potentially abusive future partners upon obtaining the green card· In the case of not wanting human interaction at all, more alternative sites provided clients with realistic life size dolls that had realistic organs and that helped them "get the steam off", providing ultimate relief to social inadequacy, sadomasochistic tendencies and member-judgment-worries.

Social Media brought up a form of online interaction based on multi-interest platforms where people were able to portray themselves as they wished. With that we saw a rise on portrait photographers who learned the wonders of lighting via filters and birthed the perfect self-made portrait called the "selfie", which often times consisted of using a pole called the "selfie stick" and looking to the side as if someone else had taken the picture. Instagram was used for pictures (mostly for exposure of body parts like the "bambi pose" or commercial shots of day to day adventures like testing food, freeze-frame dancing shots or historic relics that demonstrated the person had money to see the world on an airplane, boat or car). Youtube was for videos, day to day tutorials and even entire critics of other channels. Facebook was the never ending loop of social trends and social media activism that repeated itself over and over again via what was called the News Feed and so forth. With Snapchat (another social media application), a person could actually change their features to look like a man, woman, squirrel or cat all in real time. With that, there was also a trend called the "furry trend" where one could purchase socks that had synthetic animal hairs in it to look like paws and even have manicures with fake fur to look more unique.

The downside was that while: the externalized version of a virtual reality celebrated the co-creation of an entirely imaginary reality but nonetheless creative co-creation of sub-worlds, it also fueled insecurity at the core level of humanity and encouraged competition. Everything was based on: virtual pokes, emojis (cartoons expressing emotions), likes, subscribes, and comments. People learned the true potential of a "thumbs up". Social Media brought upon the popularization of the term "haters", while *it simultaneously breeded each cult individually by adding the letters ER in the end· That's right! You were a youtubER so your "followers" were called CarolinERS (in the case of your name being Caroline, for example)· Soon enough, skilled people at their profession were replaced by "instagrammers" and "youtubers" at jobs (especially creative ones because of their massive followings)· Industries recruited them via the web to grow their brands quickly, to A list their projects and in an anticipation to secure their million-dollar earnings, whether they were selling crap or not·*

*The way we related to each other changed, it was tainted with comparison and bitterness· Social media started making us handicapped on human emotions and authentic relating because it encouraged us to stop developing our social skills altogether and base our entire lives on the false security of angles and screens· In the workplace, people skills like empathy were replaced by things like "neuro-sales" in order to* sell products more effectively, exclusively via the use of hypnotic patterns and manipulation of people's voids and emotional triggers and a lot of people got rich from selling these "ways of the future" that were slowly leading humans to the path of apathy and voluntarily robotization· These people were revered as "gurus" in their respective "field of success"·

The impact of emotional amputation replaced by shallow interaction, was that relationships became ordinary conveniences· Romantic partnership became a grocery list where we could go "shopping for partners" via apps and later replace them for newer apps that filled other kinds of voids like "Get your empowered quote of the day"· At first with the Ipod, people would walk around trafficked streets wearing these little white earbuds with the cable hanging over their front chakras, but as social media rose, people became more and more disconnected from each other, not even relationships were fulfilling anymore, dinner tables were filled with *phones and alerts, because social media showed us that humanity at the core: was feeling extremely lonely and secluded from themselves and each other· In that sense, we were carving our own extinction willingly, each time we fed a new dysfunctional trend out there·*

## Therapy at "Happy Hour"

*Due to the polarity-based reality that is characteristic of planet Earth, humans and lightworkers are undoubtedly bound by emotions. Emotions are streams of anchorable energy which have the ability to either set a high vibration in motion (love) or a low one (fear). Out of these two polarities stem all major human emotions accordingly: on the higher spectrum in the form of joy, peace, harmony, acceptance, willingness and so forth, whereas on the lower in the form of pride, anger, desire, fear, guilt sadness and shame. Emotions are the first form of elements within that are uncontrollable, that carry a particular density to ground humans on 3D Earth and that will eventually need to be mastered in order to reach self-realization.*

*However, the path to mastering these emotions is never an easy one nor the most pleasant one. Therapeutic modalities that provide relief with emotional overload, range from energy protection techniques to conscious tapping movements that free up pent emotion, accompanied by affirmations and of course, psychoanalysis (a sequence of hearing your own thoughts over and over again, in order to retrieve your own answers from the comfort of someone else's couch)· The real work comes from accepting both higher and lower emotions, but keeping them separate ensures popular clinical healing modalities are able to remain on the top of the list· In older practices like shamanism, it is expressed that entity removal helps, but only when one is aware that thought forms can create new entities until the core of the trigger is healed or released (the trigger holds the key because it is what sets the emotion in motion)· Humans are here to remember that they are in fact LOVE· In order to accomplish this, they must go through innumerous trials and tribulations of repeated bouts of pungent fear to successfully transform their outer shell into an enlightened state: by letting their higher self or aspect of the soul that rose higher and overlooks it all, to lead their lives so it can be based on conscious and* sovereign manifestation·

Therapy, although it has been expanding, does provide some form of the relief at the cost of codependency, meaning you experience healing on one hand, but you become handicapped on the aspect of finding your own path, walking it and healing yourself· Yet, I find that humans find very comforting to walk through the shadows of their private underworlds in groups, so outside the psychoanalyst's chair, we find a variety of therapeutic scenarios which humans go to when "shit hits the fan" (when their Pandora box has been unleashed out in the open due to some form of loss or repeated loss which triggers grief, desperation and that confronts them with an overload of emotion)·

**Fishing:** Groups of men have embraced for centuries the activity of spending time in nature· Some of them go camping, hiking or swimming with sharks· Nonetheless, a tradition that has been kept for a long time is the activity of fishing· It does not occur in the same capacity of dating where people refer to potential partners as fish and engage in various social or organized activities to get a "good catch", it is literally the action of going on a boat with some bait and sitting for hours in some lake looking for fish· From an outside perspective it seems to give them comfort, to know that they are all out there by themselves connecting to the Source of all and harnessing strength through patience· It is there in that stillness and solitude where they bestow their cares and worries into the bigger pond that they are a part of and allow themselves to simply be·

**Beautifying:** For women, the longest-sustained therapy ritual varies a bit· Women tend to find comfort by being in groups of women in special pampering centers called spas, beauty salons and waxing centers· Despite the third one (waxing center) being more like karmic therapy, women enjoy uniting in these special places that perform body rituals· They get their feet rubbed, their nails trimmed and their hair colored and ironed·

*In general, women go to these places as well as shopping malls when they are needing a day off from their responsibilities· They find that someone performing these services allows them the time to relax, although slightly more masochistic than men, because most procedures done at these centers even what they call a "deep tissue massage", can be a very painful experience· Not the mention the use of apparatuses like tweezers, curling irons, cuticle removers, files and toxic fumes that come out of nail paints used to beautify the hand, but women look past all of that in order to feel cared for, for a few minutes or hours·*

*These are the most contrasting scenarios I could sort out here and they certainly have their variations, especially during the time of higher education where groups of men and women are divided by sororities/fraternities and they each have their specific means of engaging through an assortment of bonding rituals· That's not to say women don't go fishing and men don't go to* spas, but this book is about the collective patterns that are more prevalent in modern day society· Men still go to brothels to find comfort through paid sexual activities and women still work to fulfill men's needs in order to make an independent living, for example· The only difference is that men have also taken up those roles in order to fulfill women and they are called "male companions"· The important thing is that when traditional therapy is rendered useless, humans can get very creative with where they get their alternative therapy and there's no better therapy on this planet than the world-renowned "Happy Hour"·

Happy Hour is a time-controlled-offer held at bars, eateries and taverns which provides discounted liquid spirits that can sometimes be mixed with juices and called cocktails· Unlike fishing or the spa, it does not separate women from men and in fact prizes women for bringing men, by giving them free drinks all night on the "Ladies Night" event· Unlike dating sites, Happy

Hour does not subject one or the other to fishing preferences or waxing needs, it simply provides a neutral place for bonding where people are able to maximize the use of their small salaries in a set of drinks that will provide them with instant gratification for a while· The gain is the glory of being able to live in the moment outside of their hectic lives, gathering bait for a future New Year's Date and bonding time with their loved ones· When all regular interaction outside of the bar fails, they also have the opportunity to bond with complete strangers over the bar rail where there's TVs and an in-house therapist called the "bar chef" or "bartender"·

Bartenders have been here since the beginning of distilling the first spirits and they are highly trained individuals that escort people through the various stages of life and inebriation· Some will even call you a hired driver called the "uber" at the end of the night, so you are able to get home safe without getting a DUI (Driving Yourselfhome Irresponsibly)· They hold steady their multidimensional memory, because they are able to attend to many people grieving while uncorking bottles, refilling water glasses and keeping up the tabs at the bar· They are good listeners and have seen it all, very much like our taxi drivers who are another form of therapist and drive people places and give them heartfelt counsel on different aspects of life like career, relationship, family, etc·

So in reality, the best therapists are like the shamans of the planet: the ones that had to jump into the water to learn to swim, so to speak· During their own transit of ongoing personal battles, they learned to tackle the various obstacles that limit the human experience and gained the tools needed to escort others through the process too· They are skilled at patience, empathy, intuition and taking care of other people beyond their own needs, which is what makes them so valuable· Although they are undercover, they humbly continue their life mission by working general labor jobs at the cost *of doing senseless things like "silverware roll-ups". Without them, humans would not be able to find human comfort, due to the fact that most "certified therapists" in the field of human development will always hold some form of superiority above the "patient" that was gained by a paper called: a Diploma. Did I forget to mention? Your bartender does not even mind that you show up at 2am, talk about 24/7 services.*

## Overpriced Cabin

*The popularization of Ford paved the way for a new structure of transportation composed of motor vehicles· Cars made it easier for people to get around by land, while simultaneously polluting the environment with toxic fumes· From horse and camel carriages, humanity became modernized by the early invention of a four-sided box with wheels· We stopped walking hills to exchange products and with it: inherited goodies like heart disease, a new condition called "stress" and traffic (a street malfunction that plagues the millennium with single drivers occupying 4 seat cars)·*

*With cars, came all the other forms of two, four and eight-wheel drives like motorcycles, scooters, buses and trucks· Owning a car became the second-best thing after owning a home· Entire new lines of work were created out of transportation like insurance companies, car dealerships and personal injury attorneys: whose expertise was to battle for you in court each* time you ran into an accident willingly or unwillingly. With cars came new laws like DIUs and traffic school where you would learn a set of encoded hieroglyphics and what they meant in order to drive safely, and even paid your dues via anger management courses. In the case that someone couldn't afford to purchase a car, the offer to take a lease (temporary borrowing for a few years), became a great way to have the illusion of owning a car, while half of the paycheck would go into required maintenance, insurance, parking fees, and gas.

On the other hand, for the ones that neither appreciated the possibility of owning a vehicle or in fact had no means to afford one, "public paid transportation" was still available in the form of trains, subways, taxis and buses. Trains were still viable ways of transport for the outskirts, but it was mostly subways (underground stations that connected big cities) which enabled people to get from one corner of the city to the other. Buses usually had specific pick up stations and took longer due to a set of protocolary stops which made it very much like a school bus: dropping one here and picking up another one there, with the only difference that in the latter years we actually got to ride buses with different races, ethnicities and sometimes pets too, unlike earlier times of oppression· When it came to longer distances however, buses were a bumpy ride to something as little as a nearby city, making them 3 to 4-day rides to get to the destination, in addition to some sleep deprivation and sharing common germs with other passengers due to little to none fresh ventilation·

When it comes to transportation by sea, things shifted quite a bit from the time pirates would immortalize the ocean and sack the shores· Travel in a luxurious cruise is available and ranges from three digits to higher, which enables a person to experience a couple or more locations where they get to do some sightseeing, while having a real-life casino, artistic performance venue, eatery and 24/7 cocktail hour all on-board. Cruises are mostly for entertainment, while the only true remaining offer to travel by boat is at the boiler room of a small boat (if you are fleeing a tyrannical country), or by cargo ship: a trip where you travel with workers and manufactured goods around the world taking three times longer, due to negotiation pit stops and delivery intervals.

So how did we find the means to transport ourselves for business and leisure at the same time? According to the ultimate favorite Wikipedia: The Wright Brothers finally put into motion all the hallucinations Master da Vinci had suspected a whole 'nother century earlier and put together the first functional airplane. An aircraft able to travel with actual people inside of it at a limited capacity at first, but later growing into giants like the Airbus or Boeing, which could not only hold passengers and their luggage, but a whole crew with food on cargo, beverages (alcoholic and non) and even cabin room for pets: all for a price. Some "cheap flights" stand for having to take a few stops in between each journey via "connective flights", where one can stop at a foreign airport and eat, go to the bathroom and sleep in the waiting room, while others are way cheaper: as long as you are willing to take a smaller seat, bring your own headphones and pay for goodies like lunch and your seatbelt. Flights across the world can take over a day to complete and the jetlag (dissociative disorder due to linear time jumping and sleep deprivation) is the greatest souvenir, all because most people can generally only afford to travel in economy (savings) status.

The thing with air travel is the hierarchies of high class and coach seating. Some travel in comfort while others should be grateful they get to travel at all, that is if they are able to get some form of documentation like a passport or a visa issued (not everyone is entitled to travel by plane despite of having the money for a ticket). Beneath the surface of air travel, we find the underworld: entire crafts built to serve the exclusivity of millionaires in its entirety, those get to sleep in beds and have private chefs all the way to their final destination, while general plane travelers get to eat a microwaved 10 inch meal with salty snacks like pretzels, with the hopes of sleeping on top of each other's shoulders, and thriving within the only benefit of some more "legroom" (for an extra fee) in order to be able to do some leg shifting during the ride between utter numbness and slight relief·

You can either travel to see your loved ones by land, sea or air, or...pump up the phone credit, get some wifi, skip the lines and rock some "Facetime"· Ultimately, when it comes to modern transportation: is it evolution compared to horse carriages? Absolutely! At least we are on the earlier stages of eradicating animal cruelty· That within itself speaks great volumes about humanity evolving for the better·

## All-Whites Routines

*The pains of being human*

*Despite of fear and disempowerment being the prevalent tools of the 3D (3rd dimensional physical reality), a set of rituals helps solidify the postures of giving power away to outside sources. Religion, politics, employment, and academia, being the main sources of indoctrination for humans to surrender their will without their conscious approval. The system encompasses a very simple modality in which everything is interconnected to ensure humans are enslaved within the constraints of what the power source desires them to believe about themselves: either that they are bound to be ill as old age approaches, that they are bound to spend all of their earnings in taxes, that they need school to be successful and that corporate jobs are the only way to earn a living. The underlying motive as to why keep people chained to a collective fate instead of allowing them to safely develop their individualistic traits is*

41

because the collapsing rulers of Earth don't benefit from what is known as "entrepreneurs" and "hippies", people who adopt an alternative lifestyle either off the grid or off the corporate wheel.

The interconnection of the power-submission dynamic gets established at birth when newborns are given a birth certificate and later a social security number. If they obtain one or multiple citizenships, these "privileges" are bound by rules that range from paying taxes to attending "jury duty" and going to war under false nationalism incentives, to fight for the government's private interests. They are offered the possibility of private and public schools as early as age 5, with the only difference that in private schools (although expensive), children are guaranteed a future and in the public schools, children are exposed to shootings and crime due to a lack of proper safety measures that result from lack of funding.

Children spend about 8 hours a day inside

classrooms, changing classes upon Pavlov's bells, to ensure they take all the conditioning in through repetition. With each year the critical mind becomes less active and more prone to manipulation, finally breaking into submission. Every subject is either useless or reduced to its more distorted version like history: which encourages children to accept that gigantic pyramids were made by men under slavery or skilled worker agreements, carrying almost 3 million stone blocks individually and using ramps up and down the Nile River. College or University on the other hand, is composed of supposedly more exclusive subjects like "digital marketing" and "economics" that give social status but are irrelevant when the electricity grids go off and the monetary system is dismantled.

The ritual that follows is marriage, another form in which state robs people of their rights and wants to tax them for choosing to have shared lives. Depending on your given culture, you are to perform a set of colonial traditions and be held accountable under some form of authoritarian supervision like a priest, rabbi or court representative· After that, the couple is allowed to throw a grand party for guests that only go for the food and beverage benefits, which secretly bet on how long the marriage will last· Florists, fashion designers, estheticians, wedding therapists, catering companies and venue associates all gather around your 30,000 dollar budget to ensure your "big day" will be unforgettable· After that, you are to drift off into some exotic town or island to what is known as your "honey moon"· This is the first official chance for you to make your first baby without having your guests know you did not marry a virgin·

A whole nine months later, newlyweds could have ended up with their first child which will require added expenses since the "what to expect when you are expecting phase", starting with diapers, baby formulas (in the states where mothers are not allowed to feed their children their own *milk) and vaccinations that will tamper with their immune system since infancy. Playschool, nurseries and finally kindergarten, all prepare the child for the bright future of "fitting in" and give them the resilience to "fight for what they want" in a system that is designed to screw them over and instead reward those who settle for the norm of "less and less" with things like extra security in the form of permanent surveillance.*

*By mid-age, most humans will have experienced some form of tragical-set-of-events leading to a midlife crisis and fall into the illness called "depression" (a human response to consistent overwhelm with one's environment and one's own dissatisfaction). Divorce, disease and debt age humans into dreamless beings, solely focused on day-to-day survival tasks which are senseless in nature, but that maintain a sense of normalcy during chaotic times. These tasks include: putting gas in the car, food prepping and doing laundry, among many more. With so many* restrictions, humans divide every aspect of their lives into "all white routines" for example: separating their white garments in the washing machine from the color ones so they "last longer"· These routines imply a level of mechanical functioning that is confused for shelter, but it almost tells the story of how humanity lives in a constant bore: always on the hunt to preserve human life either through spending money on miraculous serum therapies of youth, or outsmarting death itself by living beyond one's means with the use of numbered plastic cards·

Life doesn't shift much from then on unless they are able to stay content with what the system provides as life expectancy references, or if they have in fact managed to save enough money to build their own business, build their own bunker and live by one's own rules and in collaboration with others· While time goes by, humans have the benefits of social media memes to distract themselves and unlimited access to Netflix-

*Binging for only $8 dollars a month. Machines taking over our lives and the concept of "smart living" does not necessarily mean ecological, it simply means we are always monitored. The ones that noticed the dysfunction, make big creative statements: like removing the wifi from their public establishment, hoping that people begin to connect once again, without the need for earbuds or screen fixation.*

## Money over Mind

*As natural scavengers, us humans, have always resorted to some kind of compensation: a beauty that lies on the eye of the beholder. Making treasures out of trash or trash out of treasures, we thrive in the creative process of exchanging goods. This is prominent till this day due to the fact that we still hold relic establishments standing like antique stores, pawn shops and auctions. Our "valuables" have become an important part of our existence in the form of attachments, especially in a world where the rich get richer and the poor get poorer. We hold onto every last bit of material good in order to prove to others and ourselves that we are not in fact: insignificant. Having ownership over something is empowerment in the XXI Century and in the case of no physical goods being available, people thrive in possessing their own children like objects, molding them into the extension of their deepest fears and frustrations.*

*It goes out to tell you: we are so powerless that*

we get our sense of power not from inside, but from molding our external circumstances by exerting will over them. This can surely be a positive when it comes to manifesting, but it has to be subsequent to riding ourselves of greed, deceit and manipulation (which is sold in self-help books under the name of "persuasion"). We are powerless because our entire system is built on "currency", which unlike its name suggests does not naturally flow like a current but rather presents itself as a form of punishment and restriction called "money" that everyone is indebted to. Indebted to? Yes, for every cent you make out of your hard work, you pay taxes, groceries, housing, etc. In other words, money is the chips via which you play at the casino, so you have no money? You can't play, you are off on your own, at some street corner and depending on your surviving humans to help you get by another day.

From the times of kings when men claimed the land upon some divine birthright based on blood *type, until today, where presidents rise to the top via controlling the people's minds with euphoric speeches of change, the power at play has chained humanity to the tool that has fulfill their agenda for them, via money· Money is the form of Holy Grail that has the added properties of: peace of mind, false independence, and even serves as an extension of self-worth· The perfect incentive for crime, which under lacking or greedy hands leads to cheating, stealing, and ultimately murder· The perfect vehicle for us to kill each other voluntarily, under the right limitations·*

*With the money system, came the credit one, generally because the 3D matrix thrives on anchors (grounded associations) and minions (middle men and soldiers)· The more participants whether willing, unwilling, conscious or not playing the cards, the easier it is to program people that: "those structures are the way things have always been and always will be"· Insurance companies play a part in making sure that a person never really owns a home, a motor* vehicle or a business, despite paying them monthly fees to keep the protocol of having their property "protected" from "potential damage/threat in the near future". Loan systems encourage people to take advantage of "asking for help" with the potential of later being dragged to bankruptcy when the interest fees become unpayable and of course: credit cards are the perfect lender to all of your financial needs that will give you the temporary high, which you will not be able to repair at your low, as well as the predecessor of the microchip (where it is expected that everyone becomes a number that can be easily eradicated via the push of a button).

The basic structure of manipulation via numbers is how we make our important life decisions, because at some point we ought to believe that money equals value, and that value is: whatever is most convenient or triggers the collective subconscious fears of survival more effectively at that moment. This is why we see money associated with family for instance: without money you can't fend out for your own. Discounting plays an important role in making money attractive as a form of added value to one's life, suddenly giving the illusion that something that previously appeared unobtainable is now accessible. It's all about denying and granting access to limited expressions of "freedom" which pave the way to either more slavery-indoctrination, or acceptance of newer structures like taking bank loans to purchase a house. The most distinctive form of discounting is not only coupons, BOGOS (buy 1 get 1 free treats), but the national holiday of Black Friday, where stores are crowded as early as 2 in the morning, filled with camping people who fiercely wait for a branded store to open the gates to storm in, in order to purchase...what exactly? The latest TV? Which according to the publicly disclosed policy of "planned obsolescence" from tech companies, clearly states that a product is designed to crash within 2-3 years. Faulty on purpose to make you buy more, yet who could believe that? When the commercials made for these products are filled with young people or attractive senior citizens staying current·

And what is this craze snowballing to? It's all about making people so attached to technological devices, that not only will they accept to make their personal property or haven a "smart home" which monitors them all day, but also to be willing to be the guinea pigs to microchip themselves out of their free will· In other words, the more robots we are sold, the more we are being told: we are soon to be one of them· It's all groundwork down here, you know how it works! The grooming period is the most vital step for all the oppressive doctrines to materialize·

To survive in this reality, you can either become a conscious renunciate and find kindred up in the Himalayan Mountains, or you can find your way into the race, job to job and paycheck to paycheck, putting all those childish fantasies called dreams on the back burner because they *told you they were useless. And just like that: money is the badge we wear when our internal structure has been absolutely severed from our soul, that we need an artificial construct to boast. It ultimately results in money becoming the ultimate destination to accomplish normal-hood and fulfill convention, but who can blame us? We have not yet seen another way to live, without having to pay for every breath we take.*

## The Rush to Reproduce

*Part of sustaining the campaign of the American Dream is leaving human bundles in the world. This is portrayed as the ultimate fulfilment: extending one's last name. It consists of capitalizing the genes of ancestors, without the slightest awareness that under the soul recycling feature, (predominant of the $3^{rd}$ dimension on Earth) those souls are ancestors themselves coming back in the form of children, to impart more karma with newly established roles, in which we play out the same scenarios of abandonment, punishment, and redemption.*

*The baby boom industry encapsulates all forms of memorabilia to induce the need to have children, ranging from baby products to benefits like childcare and welfare, yet that's only the tip of the iceberg. Upon creating the need in people to go into a partnership and seek to own children like pairs of shoes, the territory of IVF, hormonal treatment, egg freezing and sperm-saving facilities, introduce the real market of "having babies"· It works pretty much like shopping for groceries, having the worst case scenario be to actually rent someone else's womb and pay her to carry your child as a surrogate: a woman that will carry a child (with or without your genes inside of her), implanted in her by an artificial object, to be torn from her at the moment of birth, in hopes of one day having some form of indirect co-parenting participation as a nanny in the child's life·*

*Within the polarity it entails: wanting to "make children" and outsmart any odds of being sterile with numerous diet changes and even specific schedules/poses to mate, millions of children are abandoned by the minute at subway stations, churches, orphanages and adoption centers· Most of these have a second chance at life if the possible parents are able to prove their financial worth (among other things) and most likely if they happen to be at the infant stages, because nothing excites a first-time parent of the American Dream more than being able to mold*

their newfound child (made or already existent)·
The older children, those that have undergone
trauma have a chance at living occasionally in real
homes through the foster care system, but most
likely abused in those homes which leads them
to either run away or get sent back to the state
facilities where they came from· By their teens,
most abandoned children have already hit the
streets, gotten into some form of drug abuse
and carry some form of arrest or juvenile record
which makes them "damaged goods" to another
human· They grow up to be criminals, all because
they were unwanted children as early as
babyhood·

Once the clock is "ticking" for the eggs to be
baked (while putting great pressure on women
to give their earlier years to motherhood so that
by midlife they are exhausted about life), the
journey of "raising children begins"· During the
"raising stages" a set of repetition takes place
called imprinting· In the imprinting phase, the
child will not discover the world on its own terms

but based on all the previous conditioning their parents had as a child, and if these are acknowledged as "traditions" they will also encompass the beliefs of their uncles, grandparents and even the idols past generations worshipped whether political, athletic or religious. Upon entering the schooling institution, the child will be programmed to be obedient and to aspire the same outcome (future) as his/her fellow contemporaries based on their age number, meanwhile passing various tests called "grades" which enable them to finally step out into the "real world" as young professionals and graduates. Under common 3D law, children will be expected to go earn a living at the young age of 18 and fend after their parents in an economy where both parents and children pay for rent in order to survive. Lather, rinse and repeat, until we are exhausted with carrying out these societal roles, but as long as we get to place at least one grandchild in the Christmas picture or have a Harvard relic at home: we might as well call it a successful legacy.

*In modern times as opposed to older times which associated women's stress to "hysteria", Postpartum Depression and FTT (Failure to Thrive) are known as common illnesses, in which both parents and children are affected by the process of birthing children without the emotional and mental resources to sustain a harmonious living environment where the child is safe, and where the mother is able to stay sane· In the less privileged areas there is an increase in reproduction, while in the wealthier communities there seems to be a lack of physical capacity to even gestate· Some have because they have nothing else, and some have everything else, so nothing really satisfies them up (other than wanting more)· In a sense, we play with human lives in order to fulfill emotional voids· Psychiatry is better regarded than Inner Child Healing and with that: we have a society of extremes that never finds contentment in what it has, but on what it could have·*

*The wonders of the 3rd reality mean that on one*

corner of the Earth people are desperately seeking to enhance their sperm count while on the corner of the same street, a child is overdosing for not having someone to look after them. This is by far one of the heaviest double-standards of the planet: this need to protect what is perceived as "my own", while having a complete disconnect to those who are in need for love, protection and nurture. This is how we protect hierarchies over protecting our people, because we fail to see who the real enemy is as opposed to who is part of our own. Our people, are the extension of the smaller communities we build based on common values, but it doesn't feel that way due to political campaigns which's aim is to exacerbate the ego with false ideas of nationalism and tyranny, to the point where we call our neighbor: an immigrant, a spick, a jew, white trash, a nigger, or a terrorist.

STARSEED RECALL ON BEING HUMAN

## The Race for "Survival"

*Divide and conquer has been a main strategy to keep humans from awakening to their true potential, one that is not harnessed by degrees, nor social convention, but that comes from unlocking the kingdom within and bringing, yes! Heaven to Earth· This birthing of a new world is not to be confused with Harry Potter and drawing magic wands, but you could say it is similar· It is about conscious participation and co-creation of a more magical world, where we collaborate with each other's gifts and everyone is acknowledged and respected for holding their space in the world· In order to do so, we must eradicate the old narrative that humans are physical beings trapped in boxes, harness the cocreation elements of thought, word, action and emotion and align with the specific timelines we choose to experience, as a collective force of individualized expressions of the same Source·*

*Instilled as a value since early schooling and what is known as "education" (a set of outdated models to live by in order to get from A to B in life, while negating the possibility of expansion true self-development bestows upon the quality of human life), competition is the bait for humans to pursue paths where the "end justifies the means". How does it work? We are led to believe we are such insignificant pieces of a massive puzzle within our own existence, that subconsciously we tend to take the co-pilot seat while leaving the steering wheel to God's will, government shelter and job benefits. Likewise, we are unable to gather the internal resources needed to fight for our basic right to be critical thinkers in a highly dysfunctional world. If we pursue our own paths, then we do it with arrogance and resentment over the trials we had to face while making it on our own, because the system does not support nor honor us for being individuals.*

*Unable to fend for ourselves sustainably, within a system where inequality of basic needs is greatly limited by the control of institution and corporations over the people's wellbeing, we ruthlessly fight each other under slogans of "political correctness", "hate speech" or "social media activism" in order to meet the primitive needs of shelter, emotional validation, food, recognition and health. Our culture teaches us that we are always somehow "behind" and running out of time either due to collective unfounded fears of old age or spontaneous panic attacks regarding extinction. What does it all lead to on a collective weight? We kill each other in an attempt to self-preserve, and when not with weapons, we do it with deadly words and lowly actions like lies, deceit and betrayal of ourselves and each other.*

*Trends play a huge role in keeping up the constant artificial need to "stay current" over long term pursuits like happiness and peace of mind. Even narratives of self-empowerment are polluted to the core with self-hate statements of running away from internal pain which lead to a lack of compassion not only for ourselves but*

STARSEED RECALL ON BEING HUMAN

towards each other· This is the era of absolute
toxicity where everyone runs away from the
uncomfortable truths that we are being dumbed
down by the second into less evolved beings than
plants themselves, who at the very least spread
their roots under the earth in order to nurture
the more depleted plants around them· We
either over give in an attempt to compensate
for internal voids or we hoard our talents from
others, because most people are "toxic and drain
your energy"·

Brought up with speeches of "never giving up"
has made us the perfect rats that run in circles,
chasing their own repetitive patterns and never
seeing change in our lives crafted by ourselves,
because we must compete for resources and
"only the stronger will survive"· Ultimately, we
are fighting a battle that is senseless because we
are never ok with who we are at the moment,
nor with where we are in life: someone is always
greater and better· We are the constant fixers
of everything around us while going around with

empty cups and vague feelings of grandiosity for every penny we save and every like we get on Facebook.

Where did our humanity go?

We traded it for social status and outside approval. We forgot we came together to explore, to share and to amplify the goodness in each other's hearts, which is not limited to paychecks and momentary gratification but that allows for seeds of life in the form of music, art, service, support and kindness. We call our loved ones toxic for having a bad day and yet endure in truly abusive situations to prove our self-worth, that is because we have placed our power outside of ourselves, our self-worth in the achievements we have in the material world and because we gave our sovereignty to whatever allowed us to feel part of the whole, when it was only another piece of the puzzle, not the whole itself.

Truth is, WE ARE THE WHOLE! You, me, our

65

brothers and sisters who leave their comfort zones in order to self-make under their own rules and who very much like Plato's cavern, come back to the tribe to tell the tale of having found bliss outside of the blinding spell of the sales pitch called: "The American Dream"· And for millennia, this glorious journey back home has not been revered as the rite of passage it is, because the wayshowers have always been labeled crazy, wild, obscene or eccentric, making waking up a very scary thing indeed, where most of us prefer to crawl back to sleep and live to see another day go by, slowly accepting the reality that prosperity is not a right but a shooting star that just like inner wisdom, can only be accessed by some people, not all of us·

Luckily, something shifted in the early 90's in the form of an Artificial Intelligence browser who monitored humanity's every move, but granted them eternal practical knowledge at the touch of a click, called Google· Along with maps and smartphones, people where not only tracked for

66

*everything they did, but were also able to demystify daily narratives with physical proof of lies, deceit, and injustice very creatively: with pictures, videos and most recently memes· The internet has catapulted massive awakenings in the form of lose documentation as well as data dumps from undercover sources, that have enabled a vast majority of us to get inspired to align to a higher timeline, parallel to growing immune to the lies they've told about this (almost forgotten) corner called Earth· Almost forgotten, because Earth was so dense in its vibration, it would keep souls trapped in a reincarnation cycle repeating their same mistakes over and over again, without the slightest notion that they were not paying for their deeds, but rather they were the sacrifice itself to keep this planet on a suffering vibration for the rest of times·*

*As we reach the end of times of the world as we knew it, gurus (or masters of language) have begun to fall for their self-service agendas, tyrannical countries have made of their survivors, immigrants to new lands and humans are beginning to retrieve their pure qualities of joy, happiness, creativity and harmony. Our future? It will be whatever we choose to co-create together, moment to moment and for the rest of times. We hold the codes, the past is behind us and the world is our playground, so play responsibly with peace and abundance for all!*

## Evidences of the 5D in the Now

*Many people are wondering how great change can come about when we are at the end of the old world, some often distrustful that imminent collapse could be a sign of hope, but it is: it means we are more than ready to replace, substitute and rebuild our world with the newfound tools of creativity, collaboration and community.*

*Because the reconstruction process is gradual and goes by layers, or else everyone would have an identity crisis at the same time, change can be found in small ventures and social projects that have significantly shifted the way we perceive our former limitations of needing to compete for resources, instead of joining forces, thinking outside of the box and asking for help. That, I would say has been the greatest consciousness shift. No more lone wolves, we have increasingly found ways to lower our burdens and have access to common rights like freedom, autonomy and financial independence not at the cost of destroying each other, but by giving out our lending hand and most importantly, accepting support from others while on our individual paths.*

*The difference between a 3D (3<sup>rd</sup> dimensional) reality and the shift into 5D (5<sup>th</sup> dimensional) reality...*

*3D is the state of consciousness where we operate under the control-based rules of fear and survival, because we are brought up in lack. It becomes a collective reality due to the anchoring of heavy density emotions such as grief, despair, strife, shame, sadness and guilt. It is the reality where we only feel powerful when we have control over something, only that "something" is always outside of ourselves. Once we lose 3D material goods like fame, money, jobs, houses and codependent relationships that hinder our personal growth, we feel absolutely powerless.*

*The process of inquiry and self-reflection, along*

with losing 3D aspects of ourselves like the ego (a stress response that determines our course of action and that is built around a traumatic moment in life where we didn't feel safe), leads to waking up to the 4D (4th dimension) known as the void, where both shadow and light are visible, both internal and external. The bridge between 3D and 5D reality is where we become aware of our disempowerment as well as our hidden talents that had to be fired up via codes catapulted by some form of 3D trauma, called abuse. Abuse leads to self-sabotage, which efficiently deconstructs the 3D template of a conditioned human. Healing takes place in the 4D state of consciousness by the active process of retrieving all the soul fragments that once suppressed our multidimensional or spiritual nature (both light and shadow aspects or conscious and subconscious mind). Anything is possible now, or at least the awareness of possibility returns.

The 5D is where we remember that we have the

power inside via higher emotions of joy, peace, and love to co-create new timelines of greater good for ourselves and with the participation of those around us who share common goals, visions and values. We always had access to the 5$^{th}$ dimension but mostly through altered states via: sleep, daydreaming, doing art or psychedelics. Having tapped into that reality of alignment and co-creation, we are finally ready to craft a world where individual talent becomes the tool to craft a greater good for all, and that is how we are changing the world: with your thoughts and my emotions and vice versa. And because it's a free will zone, we only pursue objectives out of agreement, that means that when your ideas and mine vibrate at the same level or so little as complement each other, we birth new life in the form of businesses, centers, services, babies and artistic inspiration.

And so far, this is what we have accomplished...

*"Living by yourself is overrated"*

*The idea of "owning a home" has radically changed with new concepts like sharing a space with a significant other, with friends or even with total strangers called roommates. Co-Housing extends from sharing an apartment or a room to sharing entire houses and lands where kindred souls live together in a community lifestyle, whereas co-working spaces allow for different people to work on their separate projects under the same roof for a smaller rental fee than the one owed for having an entire establishment and little profit. Those that wish to remain with their own are choosing tiny pods as homes, trailers, homes made out of recycled materials that don't impact the environment and even refurbished old school buses to live a life more according to their independent pursuits.*

*Eco-Villages present a new model of expansion where resources are shared and yet each one gets to keep their individual traits while harnessing symbiotic relationships with each other and their* environment· Hostels bring about another form of cultural exchange and expanding from what was known as student exchange programs where a foreign family would host an undergrad over the period of their studies, we have a wide variety of platforms where people can trade their services for food and shelter, doing what is known as: volunteer travel· Among these: TalkbNB where you stay with a host who wants to practice a given language, and Worldpackers where you get to stay at different venues around the world in exchange for volunteering some of your time to help the business/person with common tasks ranging from photography to preparing cocktails·

Instead of wasting money on expensive hotels, thanks to Airbnb people are willing to rent someone else's apartment/room for a few nights or even months and get a local experience at the hands of human warm-hearted hosts· We are being driven by cultural experiences more than luxurious promises of all-inclusive resorts, choosing people over things. Talk about self-correcting outdated conditioning!

"Experiences over stuff"

A rise in minimalism or having only things that you use and enjoy, has paved a new way of delighting in more important things in life like finding nurture in food, value in face to face conversation and peace of mind over property value. With that, people are also growing tired of the 9 to 5 race of piece of shit jobs and shifting into more alternative paths of entrepreneurship either in the form of online/small business models or freedom from a cubicle, embracing more and more the path of digital nomadism (a career move where you use your practical skills on the internet, with the added benefit of living wherever you have access to wifi).

Ecology hasn't really been the focus of any great manufactured product until recently where we are seeing a rise in non-motorized vehicles like bicycles and an attempt to contain the damage in the form of electric or hybrid cars· Community gardens are built to feed the neighbors and there is an increase in homemade local goods, farmer's markets, natural solutions, alternative medicine, organic products, artisan work and increasing support of small businesses over big corporations· People are concerned with wellness (the overall health of a person's mind, body and soul) and health is no longer a segregated aspect where the body pays the toll of repressed emotions· In general people are wanting to live happier and healthier lives and more willing than ever to let whatever toxic baggage hinders that, finally go·

"Passive Income"

Ditching the career is possible now, with the ability to have "transitional jobs", built upon functional platforms where people naturally deliver a service that is required and on demand, like Uber· It establishes a commercial relationship between a rider and driver· The added value of ridesharing (giving rides or riding with other *passengers) is that people get to earn some extra income while conversing with strangers, and passengers that are willing to share with strangers, lower the cost of private transportation (where not only rudeness is part of the experience of riding taxis but it brings extraordinary fees to get from point A to B).*

*In addition, when seeking support, you can create a crowdfunding campaign where you put your venture out there in the world and find backing support from real people who become invested in your cause. It has allowed the funding for many social projects which have enhanced human quality of life as well as mended the scarcity of impoverished communities who have no access to resources like water, bathing, and we even have a sleeping bus where homeless people can ride for a safe night sleep away from the streets.*

*"Children are paving the way"*

*Indigos, crystals and rainbow children flooded the Earth. These groups of souls carry specific traits* to catapult specific shifts in the consciousness from the destruction of the tyranny to bringing back the remembrance of unconditional love. They are new generations encoded with the templates of justice, creativity and love that are defying all forms of social conventions when it comes to finding one's own light at an early age and spreading kindness and compassion. With that we see: many early entrepreneur children concerned with global and local issues as well as early inventors, environmentalists, artists and activists. That old narrative that "children are stupid, and they need to be quieted down" is being replaced with new forms of schooling where the well-rounded individual is the focus, as well as raising children in harmonious homes with the values of social responsibility.

In short, negativity and fear are the anomaly that have become the norm to imprison the planet and its people. Not to sugarcoat reality with fake positivity campaigns (and more complacency), but what if I told you that "fear is the norm" means that the world as you currently know it, does NOT have any desire for you to succeed? nor to explore, to create, to be joyful, to have healthy relationships nor to start your own business, among many vital steps leading to emancipation that surely can be perceived as anarchy but are simply the liberation of individuality in the collective. They call us the rebels and we are surely a threat to any agenda of control! It's a great responsibility to open yourself to a higher expression of yourself so others may feel safe to walk their true paths too, not the ones that have been involuntarily assigned to them. And what if knowing that, instead of pre-setting you for permanent opposition or failure becomes the greatest incentive to break the pattern by daring to dream, daring to achieve, daring to try, daring to reinvent yourself and most importantly daring to believe in yourself so that you may tap into the higher forces that DO want you to succeed, be happy and free? At this point, knowing what the corrupt, screwed up, unjust and repressed looks like, I would say the greatest crossroads lies ahead: will you voluntarily choose to embody lower energies or break through them onto liberated expression of the soul's desires?

Change is inevitable and already upon us! Look around you and you will find that magic lies on the eye of the beholder. It is our ability to see beauty in the little things what crafts the early and final strokes for world-changing visions. Embrace and honor who you are right now, get rid of what doesn't serve, count your blessings and manifest more, if it doesn't feel right don't pursue it, heart over hustle, love the people you have chosen to walk the path with you, lend your hand from a full cup and never conform to "that's the way it's always been", because we are past that fear of survival and already half way into thriving.

Write down one goal for your 5D vision below and start building step 1 today, your dreams and my dreams are already creating a new world!

Happy travels...

Laura Piquero (The Queen of Duality)

## METAPHYSICS ENCYCLOPEDIA FOR HUMANS

An easy to understand set of terms for humans waking up, because the rabbit hole can often times appear very abstract and complicated...

CHANNELING: The spontaneous or conscious action of tapping into your Higher Self's multidimensional wisdom, which often times feels like other beings talking to you in the form of angels, masters, squirrels, etc.

DARK NIGHT OF THE SOUL: The process of letting yourself go, grow your beard, leave your armpits unshaved, so you remember you come from somewhere else outside of the video game. Follows the experience called "the void" which is a prominent feature of awakening, where one's life has been turned upside down on all of its primary foundations. It will feel like shit for a while, you will grieve your old self numerous times but eventually, you will be reborn and live a 1000 times better life than the one you were living before

EMPATH: Another human being who has extrasensory abilities, with the superpower of feeling everyone's emotions for them. They occasionally get cranky and need someone to listen to them because most of the time the don't know which feelings of sadness, rage, grief, frustration and abandonment are theirs, and which they might have "picked up on" from other people's radio stations

GHOST: A person who used to be human and doesn't know they are dead. Then they see you sleeping in their bed with another partner and don't get it. Due to that, they will occasionally throw stuff, mess with your electricity and move your objects around to get your attention

KARMA: You broke someone's favorite petri dish in Egypt a while back, so now you work as repair man in their business

KARMIC RELATIONSHIP: The person that will destroy your life as you know it, so that you are able to finally find yourself without the baggage and without the trauma that held you back from surrendering to real authentic love which only comes after full rebirth

LOVE: The creative force of the universe which envelops all and discards none

MANIFESTATION: You think it, you feel it, you act on it and then you see the evidence of it coming to life appear before you, which you tend to label a "coincidence"

MERCURY RETROGRADE: Astrological Halloween that happens three times a year, when all sorts of ghosts from the past resurface. Due to the distortion, your car tends to break down and flights may be delayed

NARCISSIST: A person who has an emotional grip on you by playing with the frequencies of "I love you" while simultaneously acting like "I hate you" in a back and forth motion. Their objective? To have your world revolve around them, hoping that one day you will end up believing your own needs don't matter anymore and have you question if you truly exist altogether. All because they were either momma's spoiled brat or abandoned by their Peter Pan father

REINCARNATION: The illusion of taking a one-way trip to planet Earth and other planets, which is actually a round trip with unlimited miles. One pit stop may be to play the role of an African American in 1940 and sometimes it's all the way on the other end of the world: a Chinese girl in 1800s.

STARSEED: "We are all made of stars", but the starseed is a human who actually has memories of their lives in other planets as floating silhouettes, lion guardians or football head beings. Before the recall, they often feel tremendously homesick for a remote place and don't know why

VIBRATIONAL FLU: The process of understanding that you cough when you need to be heard, that your nose runs when you have accumulated tears and your knees hurt when you have hoarded resistance in life after massive energy movements like: funerals, eclipses, full moons, transitions and solar storms

SURRENDER: When you keep wanting to steer your own wheel but you have no gas left in your car, so you put your hands up in the air and say: "_____, Take the wheel"

INNER CHILD: The little boy/girl who is trapped inside the "bad memories compartment" of your adult self's subconscious mind, at the age at which something traumatic happened that made you feel unsafe in the world, which created a trigger or stress response to behave 5, 6 or even 7 years old when you feel unworthy, ashamed, fearful or guilty

DIMENSIONS: The different radio stations of existence, which very much like Dante's Inferno have different energetic species in them, ranging from fairies to short gray beings and black silhouettes that are thought forms manifested into negative energy

3rd DIMENSION: The radio station in which humans generally live and cohabitate with other undercover agents, wearing body suits. It is very much like a video game where all the players are given scripts, but they don't know yet that they are "acting" in order to add up to the richness of creation

4th DIMENSION: The radio station where all the shadows cohabitate with the light, in a sacred rite of passage that is meant to purge and merge the polarities of both. In this part of the video game, you get notification that you are running out of lives and must cease the present moment (integrating all of your lower and higher aspects). Upon acting on it, you discover you were simply playing out a script and for figuring that out, you are prized with a new canvas in the present life to rewrite the life you truly want

5th DIMENSION: The radio station where all newcomers are greeted for graduating the 3rd and 4th dimension, because you finally remember you were the avatar, not the cartoon player. Within it, there is an absence of darkness, vivid colors and the faculty of instant manifestation: you think it and it comes about. A place of peace and harmony very much like a retirement home, where you get to choose your home, your clothes, and rejoice with the fruits of your labor. The place where babies are created long before they manifest on the physical plane. Most importantly, you no longer have to pay rent nor cellphone bills because everyone communicates telepathically

EGO: "The feather than needs scratching pattern" in your life story, which tends to flare every time you feel wounded, unsafe, insecure, abandoned, unloved and unworthy. It resorts to making you feel safe by leading you to overindulge, rejoice in the misery of others, focus on your external image rather than on your self-esteem, compare yourself, diminish your own efforts, wallow over the past and so forth. It likes to break fire alarms instead of saying what it actually needs

DIVINE MASCULINE: The integrated masculine aspect of the light, which envelops the qualities of courage, honor, accountability, honesty and reliability, and has transmuted the lower aspects of the masculine energy such as: power hunger, abuse, greed, lust and deceit

MISSION: The prominent sensation upon or prior to awakening of having a sense of urgency to do something important. You feel you are running out of time but you only know how to paint, dance, sing, read and organize things, which is probably what your mission is, simply using those gifts at a grander capacity

DIVINE FEMININE: The integrated feminine aspect of the light, which envelops the qualities of intuition, creativity, empathy and compassion, and has transmuted the lower aspects of the feminine energy such as: manipulation, shame, guilt, and victimization

TAROT: A set of cards that has archetypes and that can help get a deeper insight into the possibilities and energies that surround the things that trouble you in order to have a better understanding", a bird's eye view if you must

SPIRITUAL BYPASSING: The inability to be raw, active and truthful about the BS that is going on in the world, because the way to a peaceful world according to NEW-AGE-CONDITIONING is silence, smiling and submission, due to the fact that "we are all one"...one step from being microchipped for good

SOULMATE: A person that may look like you or not, may come from where you came from or not, but that instantly feels like home, that is, because they in fact come from your true home and they are part of your soul family

Laura Piquero "The Queen of Duality" is an artist and communicator of self-transformation with an emphasis on shadow work, emotional validation and unleashing individual creative expression. Her work is centered on embracing the awakening process through deep self-quest and self-love, where reinvention is key to retrieve our co-creative abilities. Within it all, the shadow self plays a vital role in integrating our beings back into wholeness and as such it is the axis of self-mastery itself.

The Queen of Duality Portals

Facebook: www.facebook.com/thequeenofduality
Blog: www.lauradeepthinking.wordpress.com
IG: @queenofduality
Youtube: Laura Piquero

Made in the USA
San Bernardino, CA
30 March 2020

66553869R00058